THE

K I D'S

GUIDE TO MAINE

Eileen Ogintz

Down East Books

Camden, Maine
Guilford, Connecticut

Thank you to Charlene Williams and Visit Maine, to Mel Yemma for fact checking, to John T. Kelly at Acadia National Park, and to Sharon Davis Pearson for talking to Maine kids about what they love most about where they live.

All the information in this guidebook is subject to change. We recommend that you call ahead to obtain current information before traveling.

Down East Books

An imprint of Globe Pequot

Distributed by NATIONAL BOOK NETWORK

Copyright © 2018 Eileen Ogintz

Cover image © iStock.com/primulakat (lighthouse); © iStock.com/Bullet_Chained (puffin); © shutterstock.com (bench, ice-cream cone, paddles, jumprope girl, elk, trees, crab, lobster, kids holding hands, bears, camera, ferris wheel, hot dog, picnic bench and chairs, blueberries, picnic basket, seagull, binoculars, sailboat); courtesy of designer (whale tail, shopping bags, blue bird on top of bench, the sun, canoe)

British Library Cataloguing in Publication Information available

Library of Congress Cataloging-in-Publication Data

|Names: Ogintz, Eileen, author.
Title: The kid's guide to Maine / Eileen Ogintz.
Description: Camden, Maine : Down East Books, 2018. | Includes index. |
  Identifiers: LCCN 2017050289 (print) | LCCN 2017051126 (ebook) | ISBN
  9781608939831 (e-book) | ISBN 9781608939824 (pbk.)
Subjects: LCSH: Maine—Guidebooks—Juvenile literature.
Classification: LCC F17.3 (ebook) | LCC F17.3 .O35 2018 (print) | DDC
  974.1—dc23
LC record available at https://lccn.loc.gov/2017050289

The paper used in this publication meets the minimum requirements of American National Standard for Information Sciences—Permanence of Paper for Printed Library Materials, ANSI/NISO Z39.48-1992.

Printed in the United States of America

Contents

1
Welcome to Maine!

Kayak, canoe, or paddleboard?

Maybe you'd rather hike and camp, or sail. Whatever you like to do outdoors, you're likely to find it in Maine at the northeasternmost corner of the country—even in winter, when everyone goes out to play in the snow, ice skate and ski, snowmobile and snowboard, snowshoe, and build snowmen.

In fall, you can jump in the leaves while it is still warm—and the pesky summer bugs are gone! And pick apples, too.

A MAINE KID SAYS

"Maine is really awesome. We've got the ocean, mountains, lakes, and roads to everywhere. If there is something you want to do, you can probably do it in Maine!"
—Ceila, 12, Portland

Maybe you'd like to see some art at a museum. There's a Maine Art Museum Trail (maineartmuseums.org). Learn a little history. Visit a farmers' market or a farm, or go on a Moose Safari. Climb to the top of a lighthouse or shop 'til you drop at L.L. Bean—they are open 24 hours a day! Of course, you'll want to eat some lobster!

It's no wonder families have been coming to Maine for vacation for centuries.

Maine is big—as big as all of the other New England states combined with over 5,000 miles of coastline (including its 4,600 islands), 6,000 lakes and ponds, 32,000 miles of rivers, and 17 million acres of land for hiking, biking, skiing, snowmobiling, and more outdoor fun.

Augusta

You might be able to see a whale . . . or a moose! You will certainly see plenty of birds! And don't miss trying Moose Tracks ice cream.

First, though, you have to figure out where you'll be in Maine. That will help you figure out what you'll want to do.

- **Portland:** Maine's cultural center with museums, performing arts, and lots of good eats! Take a cruise on Casco Bay!

- **MidCoast:** You'll find fishing villages, the famous Maritime Museum in Bath, and lots of places to eat seafood. You can go out for a sail on a historic ship.

A MAINE KID SAYS

"I love the fall because it's not too hot, not too cold, all the leaves turn colors, and that's when all the fairs are, with farm animals and loads of rides and the midway. The only bad part about fall is that you have to go back to school."
—Nikki B., 11, Pownal

- **Penobscot Bay:** The place to see lighthouses, lobster boats, and small beaches.

- **Acadia National Park:** Has it all—ocean, mountains, and lakes.

- **The Down East Coast:** This is blueberry territory and the place for wildlife reserves where you can hike along the coastline and look for birds.

- **The Southern Coast:** You'll find beaches, amusement parks, mini-golf, and outlet malls. Rent a bike or surfboard, go deep sea fishing or whale watching. Locals say Ogunquit Beach is one of the best. Wells Beach stretches for 7 miles and is home to the famous Rachel Carson National Wildlife Refuge. How many different birds can you see?

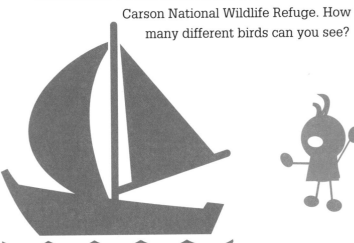

- **Maine Highlands:** Don't miss mile-high Katahdin, paddling through the wilderness, white-water rafting, Moosehead Lake, and the Penobscot River, where it's fun to fish.

- **Kennebec Valley And Moose River Region:** Home to the state capital of Augusta, the Maine State Museum, and Old Fort Western, the country's oldest stockade. If you are brave (and old enough), go rafting down the Kennebec River!

- **Western Lakes And Mountains:** Where campers have gone for many years in warmer weather and to find snow resorts in the colder months. Some families come every weekend for fun in the snow!

Where do you want to go first?

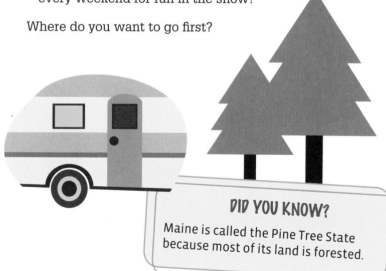

DID YOU KNOW?
Maine is called the Pine Tree State because most of its land is forested.

Maine Speak

Many expressions you'll hear in Maine come from the English, Irish, French and Scottish origins of the settlers. Here is a guide to Maine Speak, according to local experts.

Ayuh means "Yes."

Beans refers to the traditional weekend meal that always included baked beans as well as serving as an expression of someone's lack of knowledge: "He doesn't know beans!"

Camp refers to a vacation house on a lake or in the woods.

Chicken dressing is chicken manure.

"Come into the wind" means you should wait a minute.

Cunnin' means "Cute."

Mud Season is mid-March to mid-April.

"Middlin' smart, thank you" is what you say when someone asks "How are you?"

Rusticator is a summer visitor who traditionally comes for the whole summer.

"Sandpaper the anchor" would mean for grandmas to find kids something to do to get them out of the way.

TELL THE ADULTS

Whatever season you visit Maine, you're likely to find a festival guaranteed to enhance your visit:

- **January/February:** Camden Winterfest is a community ice-carving event with music, good eats, and sledding.

- **February:** Maine Lakes Winter Carnival offers sled dog racing.

- **March:** Maine Maple Sunday is always the fourth Sunday in March, visit maple syrup farms and see how the sap is transformed into syrup.

- **May:** "Moose Mainea" is a month-long celebration in the Moosehead Lake Region when the creatures are most visible.

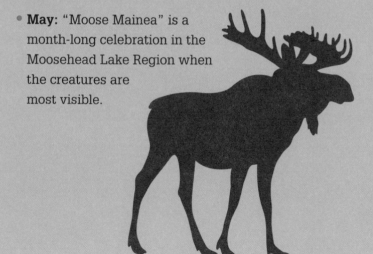

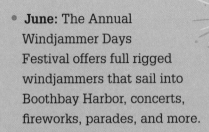

- **June:** The Annual Windjammer Days Festival offers full rigged windjammers that sail into Boothbay Harbor, concerts, fireworks, parades, and more.

- **August:** The Maine Lobster Festival is a world-famous event in Rockland that features harbor cruises, contests, entertainment, and a parade.

- **December:** Christmas Prelude in Kennebunkport features candlelight caroling, a lobster bake, and the arrival of Santa by lobster boat.

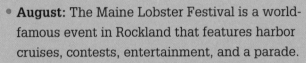

A MAINE KID SAYS

"You can get crazy souvenirs here, like bags of moose poop candy. It's just chocolates, but it's a pretty funny gift to give someone."
—Darrin, 11, Portland

Maine Inventions

Earmuffs

Toothpicks

Microwave oven

Machine gun

The original snowmobile, called a Motor Ice Boat

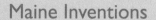

DID YOU KNOW?

The original inhabitants of Maine were Native Americans. They lived here for thousands of years.

MAINE WORD SCRAMBLE

Can you unscramble these words related to Maine?

BORETSL   _ _ _ _ _ _ _

OPBARADDDGLENI   _ _ _ _ _ _ _ _ _ _ _ _ _ _ _

EMOSO   _ _ _ _ _

SEBAHCE   _ _ _ _ _ _ _

BELANL   _ _   _ _ _ _

EBRSEILEBRU   _ _ _ _ _ _ _ _ _ _ _

NTAMIUONS   _ _ _ _ _ _ _ _ _

GUUTSAA   _ _ _ _ _ _ _

ISNKIG   _ _ _ _ _ _

CEOAN   _ _ _ _ _

See page 134 for the answer!

{ **What's Cool?** Blueberry pancakes with Maine blueberries at a Maine diner!

2

Along The Maine Coast: Water Slides, Tide Pools, and Water Sports

Welcome to Vacationland.

That's Maine's state slogan, and you'll see why as soon as you arrive on Maine's southern coast with its miles of beaches, old-fashioned amusement parks, outlet stores, and towns made for tourists. No wonder families have been coming here to vacation for generations!

The hardest part will be deciding what to do first— shop 'til you drop? Bury your brother in the sand at the beach? Zoom down a giant water slide? Eat a lobster roll?

All along the coast you'll find Maine's famous lobster pounds, where you tie on a bib and dig in to seafood chowder, fried fish, or even a whole lobster (more about that in another chapter!).

A MAINE KID SAYS

"The ocean is really cold here in Maine but on a hot day it feels great. I like to go looking for shells and sand dollars when the tide is out."

—Marta, 11, Pownal

Be prepared for crowds and a lot of traffic. This area is especially busy in summer!

Kittery is the first town you'll come to in Maine—as soon as you go over the bridge from Portsmouth, New Hampshire. Kittery was also Maine's first town, dating back to 1623. People come here to shop at the Kittery Outlets—there are over 120 shops along a 1-mile stretch of US 1. The most famous is the Kittery Trading Post (301 US 1, Kittery; 888-587-6246; kitterytradingpost.com) where you'll find everything from kayaks to sleeping bags to fishing poles. You can find water shoes or hiking boots too—in case you forgot yours!

DID YOU KNOW?

The official Maine snack is a Whoopie Pie. It's made with two round pieces of chocolate cake with vanilla frosting between them. Every year, there is a Maine Whoopie Pie Festival where bakers compete for the top treat.

But don't miss Seapoint Beach and Fort McClary, an old military fort where there is also a museum—and a great place for a picnic. You can spend a whole day exploring Fort Foster Park with places to hike, bike, swim, and explore what's left of the military fort. Kittery is also home to the Kittery Historical and Naval Museum (200 Rogers Rd., Kittery; 207-439-3080; kitterymuseum.com).

The Yorks are made up of four different villages—York Harbor, York Village, York Beach, and Cape Neddick. Check out the Cape Neddick Light Station—everyone calls it "The Nubble" (nubble light.org). There are also free concerts in the summer in Ellis Park.

A MAINE KID SAYS

"I love to go surfing, especially at Higgins Beach (Scarborough) and at Old Orchard. It's not big waves like in Hawaii but it's still really great."
—Stevie, 14, Freeport

Check out the Big A—Mount Agamenticus—York County's highest point. It's less than 700 feet, but a great place from which to see the ocean, woods, and even the White Mountains on a clear day. The 10,000-acre preserve (agamenticus.org) is huge. Fly a kite, watch for birds, and bring a picnic!

Ogunquit has a very pretty beach. Take a walk along the Marginal Way, the mile-long path at the edge of the ocean and explore the tide pools for tiny sea creatures!

Love the beach? Wells is north of Ogunquit and has 7 miles of beachfront, the Rachel Carson National Wildlife Refuge, and the Wells Reserve.

The Kennebunks—Kennebunkport and Kennebunk—are well-known as the summer home of former President George H.W. Bush and his family. The most famous beach here is Goose Rocks Beach.

{ What's Cool? Taking a ride—maybe with ice cream—on an old-fashioned trolley, bells clanging, at the **Seashore Trolley Museum** (trolleymuseum.org) in Kennebunk.

You can also go whale watching (firstchancewhale watch.com) or take a ride on a lobster boat. You can canoe, kayak, or paddleboard on the Kennebunk River (kennebunkportmarina.com).

Besides its famous long beach, Old Orchard has free concerts all summer on Thursdays at Old Orchard's Memorial Park, followed by fireworks by the pier.

Like baseball? Go to Old Orchard Ball Park (oobballpark.com) to watch college baseball and pro teams from the independent baseball league.

Got your mitt?

DID YOU KNOW?

There are more than 4,600 islands off the coast of Maine.

What's Cool? A bike ride along the **East Coast Greenway** (easterntrail.org) between Kittery and South Portland—it goes for 65 miles!

Have Your Binoculars?

You'll want them at the **Rachel Carson National Wildlife Refuge** (321 Port Rd./Route 9 Wells; 207-646-9226, fws.gov/refuge/rachel_carson).

This 50-mile refuge was established to protect salt marshes and estuaries for migratory birds. See if you can spot a Piping Plover (75 percent of Maine's plovers nest here or near here) or a Saltmarsh Sparrow.

Rachel Carson was a world-famous marine biologist and environmentalist who is credited with helping to make people aware of the need to protect the environment. Families come here to fish, kayak, canoe, and in the winter, to snowshoe or cross-country ski.

In the summer, it's all about bird watching. Visit one of the trails, like the 1-mile Carson Trail at the Wells headquarters or The Timber Point Trail, which takes you through different habitats and ends overlooking the Atlantic Ocean.

You might also want to check out the Wells National Estuarine Research Reserve (342 Laudholm Farm Rd., Wells; 207-646-1555, wellsreserve.org) with its miles of hiking and places to bird watch.

How many different birds did you see?

Amusement Parks

Maine amusement parks are not like giant theme parks. That's what makes them so much fun. The best ones, locals say, are in the Old Orchard area.

- **Funtown/Splashtown USA** (774 Portland Rd./US 1, Saco; 207-284-5139; funtownsplashtownusa.com). In Saco, Funtown/Splashtown USA is where you can ride Maine's tallest log flume ride, Maine's only wooden roller coaster, and all varieties of other water rides.

- **Aquaboggon Water Park** (980 Portland Rd./US 1, Saco; 207-282-3112; aquabogganwaterpark.com). Wear a bathing suit that won't fall off in the giant water slides. There is also mini golf, arcades, go carts, and bumper boats.

A MAINE KID SAYS

"Funtown Splashtown USA (Saco) is my favorite place in summer. There are loads of rides and a rollercoaster at Funtown and awesome water slides and wave pools at Splashtown. You can get food there, but my mom always packs a picnic and we get hot fudge sundaes on the way home."
—Nikki, 11, Pownal

- **Palace Playland** (1 Old Orchard St., Old Orchard; 207-934-2001; palaceplayland.com) is the biggest in the area, with more than 25 rides, including a fun house, roller coasters, and huge arcade.

- **York's Wild Kingdom** (1 Animal Park Rd., York; 207-363-4911; yorkswildkingdom.com) is New England's only combination zoo (have you ever seen a Kookaburra?) and amusement park with a Butterfly Kingdom, haunted house, mini golf course, batting cages and plenty of rides for the youngest park goers.

DID YOU KNOW?

Old Orchard Beach's pier (2 Old Orchard St., Old Orchard; 207-934-3595; oobpier.com) juts right into the ocean from downtown and has been there for more than 100 years. There are arcades, restaurants. and shops on it that you can visit.

TELL THE ADULTS

Beaches and pools are a lot of fun, but they can be dangerous. The American Red Cross has developed a free swim app (redcross.org/get-help/how-to-prepare-for-emergencies/mobile-apps) to promote water safety, including safety-themed games. The vast majority of drownings occur when children aren't being supervised and they can happen in seconds.

- Designate one of the adults to be a "water watcher," even if there are lifeguards on duty. Stay "touching distance" to preschoolers and toddlers around the water.

- Make it a rule that older kids swim with a buddy.

- Don't rely on water wings or other inflatable toys. When boating, insist everyone wear Coast Guard–approved life jackets.

MAINE WORD SEARCH!

Find and circle the two hidden words related to safety!

Nubble Light   Kittery   Blueberries
Vacationland   Lobster   York
Moose   Agamenticus   Binoculars

```
N  U  B  B  L  E  L  I  G  H  T  F  B
S  U  N  S  C  R  E  E  N  A  O  N  L
C  F  K  I  T  T  E  R  Y  G  U  A  U
V  A  C  A  T  I  O  N  L  A  N  D  E
E  L  N  P  D  I  V  U  T  M  T  I  B
T  Y  O  R  K  B  F  M  L  E  C  A  E
M  U  M  B  R  E  L  L  A  N  R  O  R
O  A  T  Y  S  A  M  R  D  T  H  T  R
O  I  I  P  J  T  C  E  Y  I  R  D  I
S  D  R  M  T  Y  E  L  Z  C  X  T  E
E  F  E  T  I  L  A  R  S  U  N  V  S
B  I  N  O  C  U  L  A  R  S  Q  P  N
```

See page 134 for the answer!

3

Lighthouses,
Windjammers, and
Good Eats

What are you going to do first?

In and around Portland, Maine's biggest city, you can go biking or hiking or cross-country skiing in the winter. Everyone loves the Eastern Promenade Trail! Head out on Casco Bay for whale watching, take a ride on a lobster boat, or go sailing. Join local kids rooting for Portland's minor league team, the Sea Dogs. The website visitport land.com is a good place to help you plan your visit.

Portland also has been home to famous people, including the painter Winslow Homer, especially famous for his seascapes. You can see some of his works at the Portland Museum of Art (Seven Congress Square, Portland; 207-775-6148; portlandmuseum.org) and arrange to visit

DID YOU KNOW?

Portland is on the East Coast Greenway, a huge network of trails for biking, hiking and in the winter, cross-country skiing and snowshoeing (trails.org).

his oceanfront studio. Bring along a sketch pad and see if you get inspired! Stop by the museum's workshop, which offers lots of art projects you can do, and pick up a Wonder Wheel so you can play games in the galleries you visit.

Do you like poetry? One of America's most famous poets, Henry Wadsworth Longfellow, was born in Portland and you can travel back in time to when he lived here as a child more than 200 years ago at the Wadsworth-Longfellow House (489 Congress St., Portland; 207-774-1822; mainehistory.org).

A MAINE KID SAYS
"I am all about the Portland Skate Park in summer. Most of the people there are pretty chill and there are some amazing skaters, like myself of course."
—Ty, 12, Portland

See what life was like for the four boys in a sea captain's family in eighteenth-century Maine at the Tate House Museum (1270 Westbrook St., Portland; 207-774-6177; tatehouse.org). How would you have liked to live without electricity—or WiFi?

Portland, in fact, has lots of museums—perfect for a rainy day or one that is really hot or cold—whether you are interested in trains or theatre, hidden animals (do you believe in Bigfoot?) or stars.

Before you go, take a digital tour online and see what you don't want to miss. Also check out if there are special

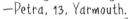

A MAINE KID SAYS

"Every summer my cousins come up from Virginia and we all go on a whale watching trip. We've seen humpbacks, minkes, and once there was an ocean sunfish sunning itself on the surface. It was so bizarre-looking, with its big eye looking up!"
—Petra, 13, Yarmouth.

family programs happening when you will visit. Here are some of Portland's museums, besides the art museum, that are especially popular with local kids:

The Children's Museum & Theatre of Maine (142 Free St., Portland; 207-828-1234; kitetails.org). Learn about where your food comes from in the kid-size farmers' market. There's also an entire kid-size town. Have you ever seen a Camera Obscura, a device that lets you dance with your shadow and make all kinds of colors against the wall? See how fast you can make balls go in the Have a Ball! exhibit. There are special playtimes for kids with challenges. Come to the theater to see a show produced for kids and by kids!

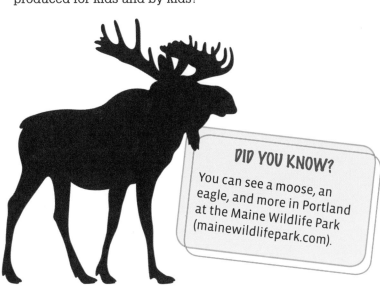

DID YOU KNOW?

You can see a moose, an eagle, and more in Portland at the Maine Wildlife Park (mainewildlifepark.com).

What do you think about the abominable snowman? At the International Cryptozoology Museum (4 Thompson's Point Rd., Suite 106, Portland; 207-518-9496; cryptozoologymuseum.com) you can see skulls and footprints that might just make you believe in creatures such as Bigfoot and the Loch Ness Monster. Cryptozoology is the study of such stories.

Take a ride along Portland's waterfront on an old-fashioned train at the Maine Narrow Gauge Railroad Co. & Museum (58 Fore St., Portland; 207-828-0814;

A MAINE KID SAYS

"Since I help my uncle lobstering, I have lobster a lot. It's pretty messy eating a steamed lobster, even if you know what you're doing. Some of the stuff inside a lobster that looks gross is really good to eat. The pink stuff in the tail is eggs—think of it as lobster caviar! And the green paste is tomalley and really good on toast. It's like pâté Try it!"
—Tommy, 14, Freeport

mainenarrowgauge.org), where you can climb onto some of the cars. (Take the Polar Express at Christmas!)

Settle in for an astronomy show at the Southworth Planetarium at the University of Southern Maine (70 Falmouth St., Portland, ME; 207-780-4249; usm.maine.edu/planet).

Visit the Maine History Gallery (489 Congress St., Portland; 207-774-1822; mainehistory.org), or visit the Osher Map Library (314 Forest Ave., Portland; 207-780-4850; oshermaps .org) with its many kinds of maps and globes and see how everyone managed to find their way long before Google Maps.

Who gets to decide what you do first?

{ What's Cool? Going to see the **Sea Dogs** (271 Park Ave., Portland; 207-874-9300; seadogs.com) play in summer—they are Portland's popular minor league baseball team.

Lighthouses

Maine is famous for its lighthouses—tall towers with bright lights at the top that were built to help maritime pilots navigate their ships to shore and steer away from dangerous rocks or reefs. Think of them as old-fashioned traffic lights on the sea. Before electricity, lighthouse keepers had to ring the fog bell in a certain pattern to help the ships' captains know where they were. The keepers also had to light lamps and rotate the lens that would magnify the light. Sometimes, their families would live with them. Portland has six lighthouses within 20 minutes of the city. There are lighthouse bike tours and lighthouse cruises. It's also easy to navigate with your family. The website visitportland.com is a good resource to figure out which lighthouses you most want to visit. Here are a few examples:

Portland Head Lighthouse (1000 Shore Rd., Cape Elizabeth; 207-799-2661; portlandheadlight.com) on the shore of Fort Williams Park in Cape Elizabeth, is located at the entrance of Casco Bay and is one of the most photographed lighthouses in the country. There's also a museum there that offers a big park to play or fly kites.

Spring Point Ledge Lighthouse (Fort Rd., South Portland; 207-699-2676; springpointlight.org) extends into the harbor from the grounds of Fort Preble. Walk out to the end of the 950-foot breakwater and take a tour of a real working lighthouse!

Bug Light Park Lighthouse (South Portland; 207-767-7299; southportland.org/departments/parks-recreation-aquatics pool/parks-department/parks-trails-beaches/bug-light-park) marks the end of the breakwater that shields Portland Harbor. There is a big park here to fly kites and picnic, or you can walk along a paved path to the Bug Light. A big July 4th celebration is held here as well.

Two Lights State Park (7 Tower Dr., Cape Elizabeth; 207-799-5871; visitmaine.com/things-to-do/parks-recreation-areas/two-lights-state-park) offers good views of twin lighthouses that were built in 1828. They are on private property but can be viewed from the park where you can also picnic, watch the ships in the distance, and take a walk along the shoreline. If the family is hungry, eat with a view of the lighthouses at **The Lobster Shack at Two Lights** (225 Two Lights Rd., Cape Elizabeth; 207-799-1677; lobster shacktwolights.com) high above the rocks.

Good Eats

Downtown Portland has more than 100 restaurants and is famous for its creative chefs who use locally grown produce and just-caught fish in their recipes. There are plenty of ethnic eats too. Try something new. (Ask for an appetizer portion or half-sized portion!) Here are some places local kids love:

For breakfast, you can't beat **Becky's Diner** (390 Commercial St., Portland; 207-773-7070; beckysdiner.com), which serves breakfast from 4 a.m. to 4 p.m. It's a local landmark on the waterfront where you can meet local fisherman, firemen, and ferry boat crews who come every day. The huge cakes and pies are hard to resist—even at breakfast.

For ice cream, **Smiling Hill Farm** (781 Country Rd./ Route 22, Westbrook; 800-743-7463; smilinghill.com) is the place to go. A working dairy farm, Smiling Hill Farm produces milk, ice cream, and more. It's close to downtown Portland and

offers onsite parking, a petting zoo, lots of barnyard activities, a farmers' market, and plenty of seasonal snacks.

Vegetarians in the family will love **Silly's** (40 Washington Ave., Portland; 207-772-0360; sillys.com), which has plenty of veggie, vegan, and gluten-free offerings along with plenty of choices for the meat eaters among you. Check out the funny names for the food on the menu!

If you want (or need) to eat on the go, **Food Trucks** (portlandmainefoodtrucks.com) offer some of the best eats in the city. Head to the Eastern Prom that overlooks Casco Bay and grab fish n' chips, a burrito, cupcakes, and more.

Flatbread Company (72 Commercial St. #5, Portland; 207-772-8777; flatbreadcompany.com) on Portland Harbor is the place to watch your pizza being baked, or call ahead for takeout and eat while taking a boat trip on Casco Bay!

For seafood, **Portland Lobster Company** (180 Commercial St., Portland; 207-775-2112; portlandlobster company.com) right on the wharf offers some of the best. Also check out the Bite Into Maine food truck (biteintomaine.com) for more options from the sea.

For tacos, nachos, and quesadillas, check out **El Rayo Taqueria** (26 Free St., Portland; 207-780-8226; elrayo taqueria.com) in a former gas station with a menu just for kids' and plenty of picnic table seating outside so kids can play.

TELL THE ADULTS

Museums, especially local ones, are great places to learn, have fun, and meet local families, as well as to get a sense of a region. Here's how to make the most of your experience:

- Take a virtual tour of the museums you plan to visit in advance with the kids. Zero in on a few exhibits and talk to the kids about what they will see—art painted in Maine, for example; a house like it was a long time ago, historic maps, etc. Find out what most interests them.

- Make sure to check if there are special family programs and kids' discovery rooms.

- Come when you are well rested and have eaten.

- Wear comfortable shoes.

- Stop at the gift shop when you arrive and get a few postcards to have a scavenger hunt through the galleries.

DID YOU KNOW?

Dozens of languages are spoken in Portland schools because many refugees have settled here.

CONNECT THE DOTS

Connect the dots to draw an animal found in Maine's water.

What animal is it? __ __ __ __ __ __ __

See page 135 for the answer!

Start

4

Freeport, L.L. Bean, and the Outlet Stores

I ♥ MAINE

It all started with a pair of damp hiking boots.

Leon Leonwood Bean came back from a hunting trip in Maine with cold, wet feet—and an idea. He got a local shoemaker to stitch leather uppers onto rubber boots that would keep his feet dry in the Maine woods. The boot—still sold today as the Maine Hunting Shoe—not only changed outdoor footwear but launched one of the most successful American family businesses. Today Shawn Gorman, L.L. Bean's great grandson, is the chairman of the board.

A MAINE KID SAYS

"L.L. Bean has a trout pond right in the middle of the store. They also have an aquarium full of Maine fish. There's even a little bubble you can stick your head up into and the fish swim right around your head. Awesome!"
—Eddie, 10, Freeport

When you are inside the giant L.L. Bean campus of stores that sell everything from boots to backpacks, canoes to kayaks, bathing suits to puffy winter jackets, towels, and sheets, you realize this is a lot more than a store. Check out the indoor trout pond and the 3,500-gallon freshwater aquarium that is like a section of streambed.

It's hard to believe that L.L. Bean started his company in 1911 in the basement of his brother's clothing shop and sold his boots by mail order. The 200,000-square-foot flagship store is on the original site in Freeport where Bean opened his shop in 1917. It wasn't easy at first. Those first boots fell apart and 90 of the first 100 he sold were

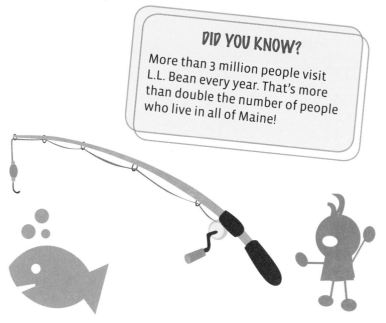

DID YOU KNOW?

More than 3 million people visit L.L. Bean every year. That's more than double the number of people who live in all of Maine!

returned. He didn't give up and refunded the purchases. Customers spread the word on his integrity and L.L. Bean's business continued to grow. Even today, L.L. Bean will take back anything the customer isn't satisfied with.

As more people started to visit Maine by car, more mail-order customers began to stop in Freeport to get gear or maybe just some advice from L.L. Bean himself. A night bell allowed late-night visitors in. That's why L.L. Bean never closes. There aren't any locks on the door either!

DID YOU KNOW?

People come to Freeport from all over the world to shop at the outlet stores.

{ WHAT'S COOL? Shopping at L.L. Bean in the middle of the night. It's open 24 hours a day every day of the year!

There are walking trails and L.L. Bean Discovery Schools to help you learn a new sport—everything from fly fishing to canoeing. There are summer camps for kids. Shoppers buy online and at outlet stores (there's a huge one in Freeport). See if you can find something monogrammed that was returned with your initials—It will be a real bargain!

A MAINE KID SAYS

"Picking blueberries takes forever because they are so small and if you keep eating out of your bucket it takes even longer. But it's pretty fun. Blueberry pancakes with maple syrup are the best."
—Willow, 11, Freeport

DID YOU KNOW?

Maine raises 99 percent of all the wild blueberries in the US.

Today Freeport has evolved into a shopping mecca with outlets for major brands from Patagonia to Gap to Nike. A lot of kids like to shop on vacation, especially in a town like Freeport where there are so many bargains. Whatever you choose:

- Talk to your parents first about what you can buy and how much you can spend. Some families save loose change in a big jar for vacation souvenirs. It can really add up!

- For a souvenir, think about choosing something you can only buy in Maine.

- Start a collection! Buy stickers for your water bottle, pins, patches, or keychains to put on your backpack.

- Don't forget a present for your pet!

A MAINE KID SAYS

"We go to Freeport for school clothes because they have lots of outlets. We get our winter jackets at L.L. Bean because they have good ones and a 100 percent guarantee on everything, so if your zipper breaks or something starts falling apart you can take it back and they will give a new one."
—Olivia, 11, Portland

Staying Safe

How did your parents get lost?

It's easy to get separated, especially in a crowded store like L.L. Bean, or in an unfamiliar town. To make sure you find each other quickly:

- Keep your parents' cell numbers and the name and address of where you are staying in your phone or if you don't have one, in a card in your pocket.

- Practice "what if" situations with your parents. What should you do if you get lost in a store, on a trail, in a town?

- If your parents don't answer a text or call, or if you don't have a phone. Look for someone in a uniform and explain you can't find your parents.

{ **What's Cool?** The World's Largest Rotating Globe, dubbed Eartha, housed in a three-story glass atrium at the **Garmin Research and Development Center** (2 DeLorme Dr., Yarmouth; 207-846-7000) in Yarmouth. The globe shows the world as it appears from space and you can get different views as you go from ground level to the third-floor balcony.

Lobster Smarts

Lobster was once so plentiful that it was considered a poor man's meal. It was even fed to animals! But that was then. Today, of course, lobster is expensive and considered a special treat. Because most of the lobster in this country comes from Maine, visitors here want to try some. You can try a whole lobster; a lobster roll, which is kind of like a salad; or all kinds of other lobster dishes, with mac and cheese, for example, or lobster served with a creamy sauce.

If you want to tackle a whole Maine Lobster, you will really need a bib, according to the website of the Maine Lobster Industry (lobsterfrommaine.com). Here's how they say you can crack a lobster in seven easy steps:

1. Watch out for the water inside a lobster—it can squirt out unexpectedly. That's why you need the bib the waitress gives you!

2. Twist off the claws.

3. Crack each claw and knuckle with a lobster or nut cracker (if it's soft enough, you can do this with your hands). Remove the meat with that tiny fork or with your fingers.

4. Separate the tail from the body and break off the tail flippers. Pull out the meat from the flippers. This is one of the easiest parts!

5. Insert a fork and push the tail meat out in one piece. Get rid of the black vein that runs the entire length of the tail meat.

6. Pull apart the shell of the body from the underside. Discard the green substance called the tomalley.

7. Open the underside of the body by cracking it apart in the middle, with the small walking legs on either side. Extract the meat from the leg joints and the legs themselves by biting down on the leg and squeezing the meat out with your teeth.

   Congratulations! You did it!

TELL THE ADULTS:
FOOD ADVENTURES

Maine is a great place to encourage kids to expand their food choices, with so much fresh fish and seafood as well as vegetables from local farms. Here's how to make food a part of your vacation adventure—and eat healthier:

- **Visit a farmers' market.** There are more than 140 in Maine, including 30 in the winter. Use the website for the Maine Federation of Farmers' Markets (mainefarmersmarkets.org) to find one near where you are visiting. Talk to the farmers and buy food for a picnic!

- **Visit a local farm or orchard where you can pick your own fruit.** Maine, of course, is famous for blueberries. Check out pickyourown.org/ me.htm and see where to go to pick blueberries in August or apples in the fall. One day in June, Maine farms are open for families to visit.

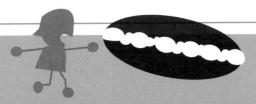

- **Try something new!** Use vacation to try foods you might not often eat at home. Search by the kind of food and location on sites such as Yelp .com, or ask locals you meet where they take their kids!

- **Order from the adult menu.** Rather than having the kids order from the kids' menu or have burgers every night, suggest they split something with you—or one of their siblings. If there are no takers, ask if you can order an appetizer or half-sized portion.

DID YOU KNOW?

Nearly 85 percent of all American lobsters are trapped in Maine—some 40 million pounds a year! It's a billion-dollar business that employs thousands of people in the state. Take a tour on a lobster boat to learn how lobsters are sustainably harvested. You'll see tours advertised in towns along the coast.

Freeport Eats

There are plenty of places for you and your family to eat in and around Freeport. Here are a few options.

For homemade ice cream in a train caboose on a farm, head to **Toots Ice Cream** (137 Walnut Hill Rd., North Yarmouth; 207-829-3723; tootsicecream.com), only 10 miles from downtown Freeport. Grab your cone and then check out the animals!

For seafood with a view, you can't beat **Harraseeket Lunch & Lobster** (36 Main St., South Freeport; 207-865-4888; harraseeketlunchandlobster.com), on the South Freeport harbor, Harraseeket's is the place to eat everything from fish and chips to lobster to a burger. Watch the lobster and fishing boats while you eat outside!

For BBQ with sauce you choose and a place to play, try **Buck's Naked BBQ** (568 US 1, Freeport; 207-865-0600; bucksnaked-bbq.com).

Edna & Lucy's (407 Hallowell Rd., Pownal; 207-688-3029; facebook.com/Edna-and-Lucys-396978543288) is the place for homemade donuts and breakfast.

Gritty McDuff's Brew Pub (187 Lower Main St., Freeport; 207-865-4321; grittys.com/pubs/freeport) offers great food and a playground! Here you can find everything from Caesar salad to burgers and pizza.

MATCHING FAMOUS MAINERS

Do you know your famous Mainers? Match the person to his or her description!

_____ Rachel Carson

_____ Leon Leonwood Bean

_____ Henry Wadsworth Longfellow

_____ George H. W. Bush

A   the famous poet who was born in Portland and lived here more than 200 years ago

B   the Kennebunks are well-known as the summer home of this former president

C   a world-famous marine biologist and environmentalist who helped make people aware of the need to protect the environment

D   this Maine resident launched a very successful, well-known business with an idea for a hiking boot to keep his feet dry

See page 135 for the answer!

{ WHAT'S COOL? Freeport's December Sparkle Celebration, including holiday tuba concert with 50 tubas.

5
Mid Coast
and the Islands of Maine

Are you MidCoast?

The answer is yes if you are somewhere along US 1 between Brunswick and Bucksport—about 100 miles.

You'll find that people here talk about Penobscot Bay, an inlet of the Gulf of Maine and the Atlantic that includes the waterfronts of many towns here, such as Rockland, Rockport, and Stonington. It was named for the Penobscot Indian Nation, which has lived here for more than 10,000 years in and around the bay and river.

Stop in at Penobscot Marine Museum (5 Church St., Searsport; 207-548-2529; penobscotmarinemuseum.org) and you can learn to tie sailors' knots, steer a real ship's wheel, or climb out on a scale model of a ship's mast to furl the sail. Check out all the historic boats and see what life

A MAINE KID SAYS
"Have Bug spray! The black flies and mosquitoes can be so bad some summers when you are hiking and they can drive you crazy."
—Ryan, 12, Freeport

was like for the sailors, boat builders, fishermen, and their families who lived here generations ago.

Like quirky stores? Then you'll love the Liberty Tool Company (57 Main St., Liberty; 207-589-4771; liberty toolco.com), which has everything you can imagine—antique and used tools, old magazines and postcards, vinyl records, toys, and dishes. Across the street, the Davistown Museum (58 Main St. #4, Liberty; 207-589-4900; davistownmuseum.org) showcases all varieties of hand tools. It's hard to believe what was built with them!

DID YOU KNOW?

Harpswell has more shoreline than any other town in Maine. There are many scenic coves and places to go fishing and sailing. harpswellmaine.org.

Maine has 4,600 islands, most of them uninhabited by humans, though you can stay overnight on some.

Window shop and watch the boats come and go in the pretty towns of Camden and Boothbay, known for their harbors. Make sure to take plenty of selfies—when the sun's out!

Got your sketch pad and binoculars? Visit one of Maine's pretty islands famous for bird watching and for artist inspiration. Use the Maine State Ferry Service (207-244-3254; maine.gov/mdot/ferry) to get to The Fox Islands, so named because an explorer centuries ago said he spotted gray foxes here. You won't find any foxes today, but be sure to check out the Vinalhaven Candy Co. (35 W. Main St., Vinalhaven; 207-863-9904; facebook.com/groups/vinalhavencandyco).

A MAINE KID SAYS

"I always have my sketchbook and colored pencils in my backpack. It's relaxing to sit down for a while and draw when you're out for a hike. I like trails that go through the woods and also along the ocean. It's really beautiful."

—Ryan, 11, Freeport

Monhegan, about 11 miles from the mainland, is another popular island for a day trip by ferry. For centuries it has been an artist colony—some studios are open to the public on summer afternoons. There's also a historic Monhegan Lighthouse at the island's highest point. This is a small place—only 60 people live here year-round and it's less than 2 miles long and a 0.5 mile wide.

Think you could make it around the island? Be sure because there are no cars here!

DID YOU KNOW?

American shipbuilding began near Bath in 1607. Today, you can watch the ongoing reconstruction of a 1607 sailing ship *Virginia*, at the visitor center for **Maine's First Ship** (122 Front St., Bath; 207-443-4242; mfship.org). You can also hear about the state's marine history, including how members of the Popham Colony sailed the *Virginia* back to England in 1609.

What's in Your Backpack?

When you're going hiking, biking, or to the beach, kids say you need:

- A reusable water bottle filled with water—two if you are going on a long hike. Decorate it with stickers from your trip!

- A rain jacket and extra layer—the weather can change quickly in Maine!

- Snacks (make your own trail mix!)

- Bandages (just in case)

- Sunscreen and insect repellent

- A hat

A MAINE KID SAYS
"I keep a good book in my backpack wherever I go."
—Allison D., 14, Portland

Ahoy Mates

By land or by sea? At the **Maine Maritime Museum** (243 Washington St., Bath; 207-443-1316; mainemaritimemuseum .org) in Bath, you can take a daily lighthouse and nature cruise, getting an up-close look at US Navy vessels now under construction at the Bath Iron Works. Bath is known as "the city of ships" for a reason!

Back at the museum, you and your family can stroll through the country's only surviving shipyard where large wooden sailing vessels were built and see what life was like for those who built the ship. Check out the full-size sculpture of the schooner *Wyoming*—440 feet long and with masts 120 feet high. It's the largest wooden sailing vessel ever built in North America—and a great place for a photo!

Inside, you'll find plenty of hands-on activities in the permanent exhibits. Check out more than 140 Maine-built or Maine-related boats—including a rare birchbark canoe. Have you got a favorite?

Watch craftsmen at work at the working boat shop. Get the complete story of Maine's lobster industry in the big Lobster and the Maine Coast Exhibit. Ready to climb inside a human-sized lobster trap?

Rockland

This town proudly calls itself "The Lobster Capitol of the World" because it ships some 10 million pounds of lobster each year. Maybe you'll be visiting in August during the Maine Lobster Festival! (mainelobsterfestival.com).

But there's a lot more to do in Rockland than eat seafood, including sea kayaking, taking a boat cruise or a ferry to one of Maine's many offshore islands, biking, and checking out the Rockland Farmers Market on Thursdays in the summer. Rockland is also home to some noteworthy museums, whatever your interests!

If you like cute birds, there are special kids' activities and live videos of nesting puffins at the **Project Puffin Visitor Center** (311 Main St., Rockland; 207-596-5566, projectpuffin .audubon.org).

If you like cars and trains, the **Owls Head Transportation Museum** (Museum St., Owls Head; 207-594-4418; owlshead .org) will delight with its collection of historic cars and planes. There's an annual rally and air show every August.

If you want to learn more about historic ocean navigation, **Maine Lighthouse Museum** (1 Park Dr., Rockport; 207-594-3301; mainelighthousemuseum.org) is home to all varieties of things related to lighthouses, the Coast Guard and more. Check out the foghorns and ships' bells! The **Maine Discovery**

Museum (72 Main St., Bangor; 207-262-7200; mainediscoverymuseum.org) in Bangor is also a great place to learn about such things.

If you are interested in how boats were built, the **Sail, Power & Steam Museum** (75 Mechanic St., Rockland; 207-596-0200; sailpowersteammuseum.org) is built on the grounds of a former shipyard and showcases Rockland's marine heritage—everything from tools to models. The **Coast Children's Museum** is here as well.

If you love art, the **Center for Maine Contemporary Art** (21 Winter St., Rockland; 207-701-5005; cmcanow.org) mounts all kinds of temporary exhibits. There are hands-on classes and workshops for all ages, depending on when you visit. The **Farnsworth Art Museum and Wyeth Center** (16 Museum St., Rockland, ME; 207-596-6457; farnsworth museum.org) celebrates Maine's role in American art. Here is where you'll find the Wyeth Center with works of Andrew, N.C. and Jamie Wyeth—some of them you may recognize! Join an art class, if there is one when you visit.

TELL THE ADULTS:
A DIFFERENT KIND OF HARBOR CRUISE

Historic windjammers—schooners with big wooden masts and sails—once carried freight up and down the New England Coast. They are named for their ability to "jam" into the wind. Seven are National Historic Landmarks today in Maine. They are a way for families to experience a different kind of cruising, determined by the wind. You can help with the sails or the cooking or just relax while watching for bald eagles, ospreys, harbor seals, and lighthouses from the water! **The Maine Windjammer Association** (sailmainecoast .com) is a good place to start. Most cruises sail out of Camden, Rockland, and Rockport. You can go out for a day or one night on the Schooner *Summertime*, or *The Sally* has daily harbor cruises. There's a Great Schooner Race Fourth of July week!

MAINE DECODER

Fill in the blanks of these Maine-related words to spell out the secret code!

Sno___

Mount Kata___din

Old ___rchard Beach

L___bster

National ___ark

L ___ ghthouse

Moos___

Free___ort

Stephen K___ng

Blueb___rry

___ ___ ___ ___ ___ ___ ___ ___ ___ ___

See page 135 for the answer!

> **DID YOU KNOW?**
> Past Casco Bay, the shape of Maine's coast changes. Instead of sandy beaches, there are rocky peninsulas with harbors, coves, and bays.

{ **WHAT'S COOL?** Watching lobster boat races. They begin in mid-June in Boothbay Harbor and are always held on Moosabec Reach on July 4. There are other races along the coast. Check when you are visiting towns, including Rockland.

6

Bar Harbor
and Mount Desert Island

Want to adopt a whale?

You can in Bar Harbor thanks to the Adopt-a-Whale program at the College of the Atlantic (105 Eden St., Bar Harbor; 207-288-5015; coa.edu/allied-whale). No, you can't take the whale home with you, but what a souvenir your certificate will make! And you'll be helping whale research too. The College of the Atlantic is also home to the George B. Dorr Natural History Museum with a touch tank and plenty of sea things you can touch, including whale baleen.

DID YOU KNOW?

Bar Harbor was first named Eden, but was renamed Bar Harbor in 1918, because of the sandbar that connects Bar Island to Mount Desert Island.

Bar Harbor is, of course, a great place for souvenir shopping. Haven't you always wanted socks with pictures of lobsters on them? It's also a great place to learn about sea and bird life, whether you go whale watching, go out on a lobster boat, or see tiny lobster hatchlings or tidal creatures at the Oceanarium (1351 ME-3, Bar Harbor; 207-288-5005; theoceanarium.com).

Get ready for crowds, especially in summer, especially in the middle of town packed with shops and restaurants. But there are lots of ways to have fun and leave the crowds behind.

A MAINE KID SAYS
"Go on a whale watch or go out to see the puffins!"
—Petra, 13, Yarmouth

See how many seals and birds you can spot at the Indian Point Blagden Preserve (nature.org/ourinitiatives/regions/northamerica/unitedstates/maine/placesweprotect/indian-point-blagden-preserve.xml). There are more than 130 species of birds here! At low tide, the seals will be on the rocks! Bring binoculars!

Try the Dive-In Theater Boat Cruise (105 Eden St., Bar Harbor; 207-288-3483; divered.com). You don't have to dive in the cold water—Diver Ed will with a video camera and will bring back plenty of creatures you can examine. Have you ever touched a sea urchin?

Look for bald eagles on a sailing trip (you can go out on Downeast Windjammer Cruises', (downeastwindjammer .com) old-fashioned schooner named *Margaret Todd*, or learn all there is to know about lobsters on a lobster cruise with Captain John Nicolai's *Lulu* Lobster Boat (lululobsterboat.com).

Learn more about what you are seeing with the big selection of kids' books at the unique Naturalist's Notebook (115 Main St., Northeast Harbor; 207-276-4120; thenaturalistsnotebook.com), where you'll find lots of kids' books and exhibits.

A LOCAL KID SAYS:
"Some places in Maine your cell phone won't get reception, especially out in the woods."
—Kevin, 10, Pownal

There's plenty of hiking and biking in neighboring Acadia National Park (more about that in the next chapters!), but have you ever gone sea kayaking? Coastal Kayaking Tours (48 Cottage St., Bar Harbor; 207-288-9605; acadiafun.com) has special family tours.

But there's nothing wrong with just hanging out either—in the Village Green, at the harbor, or in Knowltown Playground where outdoor family movies are shown in summer on Thursdays. Help your parents buy the fixings for a picnic!

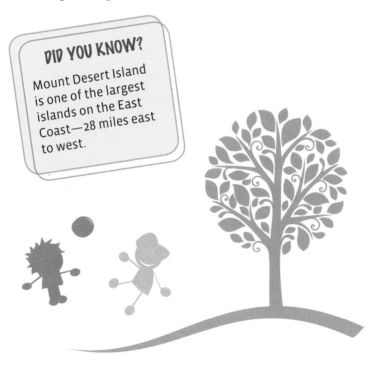

DID YOU KNOW?

Mount Desert Island is one of the largest islands on the East Coast—28 miles east to west.

Bar Harbor shares Mount Desert Island with other smaller, less crowded towns. You can hop a ferry and go to the Cranberry Islands, and before you even get to Bar Harbor you'll pass through Ellsworth and the Kisma Preserve in Trenton (207-667-3244; kismapreserve.org), which is a sanctuary for rescued exotic animals. See wolves or bears!

While you're in Bar Harbor, figure out where you want to go and what you want to see in Acadia National Park. Got your hiking shoes? Is your backpack packed?

A MAINE KID SAYS

"Bring some warm clothes with you, even in the summer. It doesn't always get super hot in summer, and especially at night you may want some sweats to hang out in if you are camping or out on a boat."
—Anna, 12, Yarmouth

What's For Lunch

Help your parents figure out what to have on your picnic, whether you need a bag lunch for your backpack or have a cooler. Try something different, maybe getting the fixings at a local farmer's market. Pick up:

- Tortillas to make wraps

- Carrots and other veggies with pita bread and hummus

- Chunks of cheese, salami, crackers, and freshly baked bread

- Fruits such as oranges, apples, and frozen grapes that won't get crushed

- GORP (good old raisins and peanuts)—mix it yourself and make it salty and sweet, crunchy and chewy with your favorite dried fruits, nuts, and candy (M&Ms always are a good bet!)

Learn the Lingo

If you are lucky, you might see whales, dolphins, or other sea animals when you are on the Maine coast. Here some common terms used in whale-watching:

Bow-riding—when a whale positions itself to be lifted and pushed by moving water

Breach—when a whale or dolphin jumps out of the water and lands on its side or back

Flukes—the horizontal lobes of the tail of a whale, dolphin, or porpoise. It's made of tissue, not bone!

Tail slap—when a whale slaps its tail flukes on the water's surface

Spyhopping—when a whale pokes its nose out of the water to look around

TELL THE ADULTS

There is plenty to see and do in and around Bar Harbor that is free or nearly free:

- **Grab the binoculars and look for birds**—bald eagles, ospreys, peregrine falcons, great blue herons, and shorebirds.

- **Hit the playground**—The Park Street Playground is where you'll find local kids and it's just down the street from the Glen Mary Wading Pool.

- **Visit the "Bar" of Bar Harbor during low tide,** the large sandbar that connects downtown Bar Harbor to Bar Island. Check out the sea life uncovered at low tide, but make sure to check the tide schedule!

- **Enjoy the Bar Harbor Town Band**—Concerts are on the

WHAT'S COOL? Thirty-six holes of mini golf at **Pirate's Cove** (368 ME 3, Bar Harbor; 207-288-2133; piratescove.net/bar-harbor), 4 miles from downtown Bar Harbor

Village Green on Mondays and Thursdays from July through mid-August.

- **Visit Seaside Cinema** in Agamont Park, an outdoor, giant inflatable screen with showings each Wednesday from mid-July through August overlooking the harbor. Free popcorn!

- **Take a walk on the Shore Path** along the shore of Frenchman Bay. There are great views of the ocean—and the grand "summer cottages."

- **Get ice cream cones**—locals such as Ben & Bills (66 Main St., Bar Harbor; 207-288-3281; benand bills.com), are also known for their chocolates.

What Do You See?

Bar Harbor and Acadia National Park are famous for their really dark night skies, which means you may see so many stars that you'll have trouble identifying the ones you know!

Can you see:

- The Milky Way?

- Planets such as Venus, Mars, Jupiter, and Saturn?

- A cluster of stars?

- A constellation you recognize?

Don't forget your binoculars!

WHAT'S COOL? Stargazing on Mount Desert Island. Three towns—Bar Harbor, Tremont, and Mount Desert have passed lightning ordinances to make sure you can best see the night skies. There is an **Acadia Night Sky Festival** (AcadiaNightSkyFestival.com) every year in September.

WHALE MATCHING

Match the word to its whale of a definition.

Flukes   when a whale positions itself to be lifted and pushed by moving water

Spyhopping   when a whale slaps its tail flukes on the water's surface

Breach   when a whale pokes its nose out of the water to look around

Bow-riding   the horizontal lobes of a whale's tail

Tail slap   when a whale jumps out of the water and lands on its side or back

See page 135 for the answer!

7
Learning About
the Wilderness in
Rural Maine

Got your water bottle?

Not a plastic one, a reusable one. It will become a souvenir once you put some stickers from the national park on it. But more important, you'll be helping the environment by creating less trash. Remember, it also wastes a lot of energy to produce all those disposable bottles and transport them to where people can buy them. Just don't fill up your water bottle in any of the park's streams. That water could make you sick because it isn't purified.

DID YOU KNOW?

There have been rangers working in the national parks for 100 years.

Countries all over the world have their own national parks that are protected by their governments.

WHAT'S COOL? Building a small tower of rocks on a hiking trail. See if you can find it on your way back!

National parks, of course, were created to protect the land and all the creatures who live on it. A visit to a national park such as Acadia is a good time to consider what you can do to help the environment and the animals who call this place home, such as the Peregrine falcons. Talk to the national park rangers about what they think kids can do.

Doing your part includes leaving what you find—rocks, flowers, leaves. Did you know it's illegal to remove any object at all from a national park? Of course you can take all the photos you want!

A MAINE KID SAYS

"For a souvenir, get a little pillow filled with pine needles and balsam fir needles. They smell so good and will remind you of hiking in the woods every time you take a sniff. Try some fried clams, or steamers if you're on a diet."
—Ryan, 11, Freeport

It also includes respecting all the animals who call this national park home, especially those whose species are threatened or endangered. Do you know the difference? A species in danger of extinction is endangered, a threatened species is one that is likely to become endangered.

Did you know it is also against the law to feed the animals? You shouldn't get too close either.

If you're camping or picnicking, you want to "Leave No Trace." That means you don't want to litter— pack out what you have packed in—including all your trash. Keep a couple of extra

A MAINE KID SAYS
"Campfires, hot dogs, fresh trout, smores! Food cooked on the fire always tastes so good."
—Aaron, 12, Freeport

storage or trash bags in your backpack! Visit lnt.org to learn more about how you can "Leave No Trace."

If you're staying in a hotel, turn off the air conditioning and lights when you leave. Reuse your towels and take shorter showers to conserve water. That's not so hard!

Get out and take a hike or a bike ride instead of driving all day. It's more fun anyway—and you might meet some other kids along the way.

Hiking Smarts

Acadia National Park is a great place to go on a hike, with hundreds of miles of hiking trails. But every year, people get hurt hiking to the waterfalls in the park. So be very careful!

On any hike:

- Stay on established trails at all times.

- Stay with the group, don't rush ahead or lag behind.

- Carry a whistle.

- If you get separated, "hug a tree" where you are and blow your whistle to alert the adults to your location. Stay there until they return.

{ **WHAT'S COOL?** Watch the sunrise in Acadia National Park, one of the first places in the country to see the sunrise each day.

Park Rangers

See the big Smoky the Bear hat? That's the most distinctive part of a national park ranger's uniform, but you probably didn't realize that rangers wear a lot of different hats—job wise, anyway.

You might meet a ranger in the visitor center or at a campfire program, where some work on programs for visitors like you. In Acadia, for example, they lead boat cruises where you can touch sea life brought up from the ocean floor, or search for seals, porpoises, and bird life.

They may also help when there are big crowds in the park. But others provide emergency medical help, patrol the park, enforce park rules, and work on fire crews. They work on the park's websites and many are scientists—geologists or biologists, for example.

Some rangers also work in big cities at national monuments, like in Washington DC, and at historic sites all over the country as well as at parks and federal recreation areas. Many have studied something like forestry, zoology, or environmental science in college. Today, no matter what their assignment, they are all stewards for the national parks.

Say thank you when you meet a ranger!

TELL THE ADULTS: LEARNING THOUGH NATURE

There is so much to see and do in nature, and so many ways to learn about what you might see.

Stop in any one of the park's bookstores (Hulls Cove Visitor Center, Sieur de Monts Nature Center, Islesford Historical Museum, Blackwoods and Seawall Campgrounds, or Park Headquarters) for kid's books about the park, the animals. and the region. You can purchase some books, patches, pins, and maps online (eparks.com/store).

Download a free Audubon guide to birds (audubon.org/app).

Acadia Quest is a series of youth- and family- oriented experiences in the park that encourage youth and families to explore, learn about, and protect national parks and other conserved lands. Families or friends create a team and complete activities in categories of Explore, Learn, and Protect. For more information, visit the Friends of Acadia website (friendsofacadia.org/events/acadia-quest).

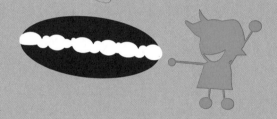

A MAINE KID SAYS

"Definitely try a whoopie pie. They used to come in just chocolate flavor, but now there are loads of flavors."
—Anna B, 12, Yarmouth

You can also use your GPS to participate in the **EarthCache Program** on a tour that will take you over much of the park (nps.gov/acad/earthcache.htm).

The **Acadia Nature Center at Sieur de Monts Spring** has hands-on exhibits to help the kids—and you—understand how the park manages its plants and animals. Have a contest to see who in the family can identify the most birds!

Junior Rangers

Ready to explore the park?

A great way to do it is to become a Junior Ranger. Pick up the official Junior Ranger booklet at any Acadia visitor center, nature center, or campground. Complete the activities while you explore the park and then stop by a visitor center to talk to a ranger and get your badge. More than 350 national parks have junior ranger programs (nps.gov/kids/jrRangers.cfm).

There are also Girl Scout and Boy Scout Ranger Programs (nps.gov/subjects/youthprograms/scout-ranger.htm).

Check out the ranger-led programs at Acadia when you visit, including a ranger-narrated boat cruise (nps.gov/acad/planyourvisit/guidedtours.htm). There's also an online National Parks Service site for kids called WebRangers (nps.gov/webrangers) with games and activities, the chance to share pictures, earn rewards, and more.

Are you ready to get started?

WHAT'S COOL? Spotting a Peregrine falcon. Stop by the Precipice Trail parking area in the morning most summer days. A ranger or volunteer will have scopes so you can watch the falcons from a respectful distance.

MAINE MAZE!

Can you find your way to the top of Cadillac Mountain?

See page 136 for the answer!

8
Acadia National Park

It's so hard to choose where to go first!

You can bike or hike, swim in icy water (even in the summer), look for birds, fish, visit an island or a lighthouse. You can even take a ride in a horse drawn carriage with Carriages of Acadia (877-276-3622; acadiahorses .com), located a mile south of the Jordan Pond House at Wildwood Stables in the park.

A MAINE KID SAYS

"We go camping in Bar Harbor and bring our bikes to ride on the carriage trails at the park. The hiking is good, too, and we always go to Jordan Pond House for popovers because my dad loves them."
—Willow, 11, Freeport

Welcome to Acadia National Park, the only national park in the northeastern US. It is the biggest national park created from land donated by private citizens who wanted this beautiful place protected forever. That's why you can visit the mountains and beaches, go canoeing or kayaking on lakes and ponds, or hiking and biking on the trails.

Most people visit in summer, though you can visit in spring and fall (check out the leaves!)—even in winter (have you ever been snowshoeing?).

Are you a fourth grader? If someone in your family is, your family can get in free through the Every Kid in a Park program from the National Park Foundation. Just make sure to download your pass before you visit (everykid inapark.gov/get-your-pass)!

WHAT'S COOL? **Thunder Hole**—as water rushes into this narrow channel during high tide, it effectively traps the air, making a huge thunder-like noise.

Make sure to stop at the Acadia National Park Headquarters or one of the visitor centers when you arrive. You'll want to check what special ranger activities you can join—and pick up your junior ranger booklet so you can complete it and get your patch before you leave.

If you get to the park really early, you might be able to go on a bird-watching walk or special kid's program to learn about tide pools and rocks. Park rangers also are on hand for evening programs at two of the park's campgrounds.

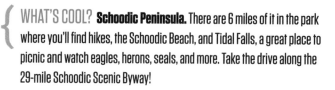

A MAINE KID SAYS

"I like the fall here. The mosquitoes and black flies are pretty much gone. It's usually sunny and warm without being sweaty hot. You can go biking and hiking and kayaking and there aren't loads of people to deal with. Fall is pretty peaceful compared to how busy summer is."
—Annaka, 14, Portland

{ WHAT'S COOL? **Schoodic Peninsula.** There are 6 miles of it in the park where you'll find hikes, the Schoodic Beach, and Tidal Falls, a great place to picnic and watch eagles, herons, seals, and more. Take the drive along the 29-mile Schoodic Scenic Byway!

Let the rangers help plan your visit. They can suggest kid-friendly bike rides and hikes. Can you walk a mile? Try the Jordan Pond Nature Trail and then stop at the Jordan Pond House (2928 Park Loop Rd., Seal Harbor; 207-276-3316; acadiajordanpondhouse.com) for a snack and to check out The Bubbles—a pair of rounded mountains to the north.

The Ship Harbor Nature Trail is a little longer and is especially popular among those wanting to see birds. Have you ever seen an Eagle?

DID YOU KNOW?

There are more than 335 bird species in Acadia National Park, making it one of the best places to see birds in the country. How many different species have you seen?

You can even hike from Bar Harbor from Schooner Head Road where the road dead ends.

If you don't mind cold water, you'll want to spend some time at Sand Beach, the park's and the island's biggest sandy beach. If the water's too cold (and it may not even be 60 degrees in summer!), build a sand creature or, locals say, walk to the end of the beach where a warmer stream meets the ocean.

Count the different ecosystems as you travel from shore to mountain summit. What's your favorite?

WHAT'S COOL? The **Wild Gardens of the Acadia** at Sieur de Monts Nature Center, where the plants are labeled so you will be able to identify them when you see them.

Taking a Hike

There are more than 125 miles of hiking trails, whether you want to climb a mountain or just head out for a walk. Here are a few options.

- **Cadillac Mountain** is the highest point within 25 miles of the US Atlantic Coast. Many people like to hike or bike to the top, especially to see the sunrise. It's 3.5 miles of hiking, but just 1,529 feet high—a lot lower than the Rockies!

- **Great Head** is at the far end of Sand Beach up granite steps. Follow the trail along the ocean's edge and take a selfie amid the giant rocks.

- **Ocean Path** starts from the upper parking lot at Sand Beach and takes you to Otter Point and back. You'll be along the Atlantic Ocean the entire way!

- **The Precipice**, if you are old enough and very fit, is the most challenging of the park's hiking trails. You'll be rewarded with seeing endangered peregrine falcons. (The trail is always closed between late March and late July when the peregrines are nesting.)

Bike Smarts

Lots of kids and their parents like to ride bikes on the Carriage Roads in Acadia National Park because there are no motorized vehicles. But accidents can still happen. According to Safe Kids Worldwide (safekids.org) here's how to keep safe on your bike:

- Always wear a properly fitted helmet. It should be snug, not rocking back and forth on your head! You can rent one if you are renting a bike. Insist your parents wear helmets too!

- When sitting on your bike, your feet should be able to touch the ground.

- Before setting off, make sure the bike's brakes and gear shifts work.

- Don't wear loose clothing that can get caught in the bike chains or wheel spokes.

- Stick to bike paths whenever possible.

- If you are on a road, ride in the same direction as traffic as far on the right side as possible.

- Wear bright colors and use lights, especially when riding at night and in the morning. Reflectors on your clothes and bike will help you be seen.

- Ride together with your family.

Wildlife Smarts

Acadia National Park is a great place to see wildlife large and small. Just don't expect to see a moose. They are rarely seen here.

Remember to be respectful when you're exploring tide pools or looking for wildlife. You are a guest in their home. Here are a few important tips:

- Don't get too close! You never want to approach wildlife.

- Explore tide pools at low tide, and don't take any of the creatures (like sea stars or urchins). And be careful! The rocks can be slippery.

- Do not feed wildlife. They won't survive if they become dependent on human food.

- Bring a pocket guide to help you identify what you are seeing, or download one on your smartphone.

- Join a ranger group for a hike to learn more.

TELL THE ADULTS

If you want to give the kids a taste of camping but don't have all the gear, consider the Appalachian Mountain Club's **Echo Lake Camp** (amcecholake camp.org) just outside Acadia National Park on Mount Desert Island. Here you and your family stay in platform tents with cots and eat family-style meals. There are boats to borrow and guided hikes, volleyball, basketball, swimming floats, and more to enjoy.

There is also **Family Nature Camp** at the College of the Atlantic, where families live in the dorm and spend days on trips led by naturalists in Acadia National Park.

Sewall Campground, one of the three in the park, on the west side of Mount Desert Island is especially popular. Park rangers offer a variety of programs from here, and Acadia's Island Explorer shuttle buses provide free service between park destinations and local communities.

Whether or not you are camping, you want to be prepared in the park, as the weather can change quickly and someone may need first aid. Here is what the experts say you'll want to have:

- jackets, fleeces, or sweatshirts

- a change of clothes for everyone (in case someone falls in the water!)

- sunscreen and insect repellent

- wet wipes and small plastic sandwich bags

- plastic grocery bags to keep trash until you find designated trash cans

- flashlight and extra batteries

- rain gear

- towels (microfiber towels are the best)

- binoculars and a magnifying glass (great to get an up-close view on the trail!)

- plenty of water and healthy snacks

- a portable charger for your phone

John D. Rockefeller Jr.

Have your carriage waiting?

You won't need it on the famous Carriage Roads in Acadia National Park, though the 51 miles of gravel pathways and granite bridges were created by John D. Rockefeller Jr. for horse-drawn carriages and have always been closed to motorized vehicles. Today, they are popular for bikers, walkers, hikers, and in winter, cross-country skiers and snowshoers.

Rockefeller, a billionaire's son from one of America's wealthiest families, was famous for developing Rockefeller Center in New York and being a philanthropist. He also spearheaded the restoration of Colonial Williamsburg in Virginia. Since he was a boy, he had spent summers on Seal Island here and he wanted to make Acadia National Park more accessible without a car. He worried that traffic would ruin this beautiful place. He began purchasing land and making designs for the carriage road system that were meant to be free of cars. He was part of the construction process and funded 16 of the 17 stone bridges that cross streams, waterfalls, and cliffsides, all designed to mesh with the scenery of the park. They cost millions—tens of millions in today's dollars. The large blocks of granite you see lining the roads as guardrails are called "Rockefeller's teeth."

You'll love going under and over the stone bridges!

CONNECT THE DOTS

Connect the dots to draw an animal found in Maine's wilderness.

What animal is it? __ __ __ __ __

See page 136 for the answer!

DID YOU KNOW?

George Bucknam Dorr is known as the father of Acadia National Park. He spent most of his life helping to establish the park, caring for it, and expanding it.

9

Mountains, Lakes, and Moose—The Kennebec Valley and Maine Highlands

Count them—46 mountain peaks,

including the state's highest, Mount Katahdin. In case you are wondering, it's 5,269 feet high, barely short of a mile. Look for those ending their trek on the Appalachian Trail—it ends with the hike up.

Welcome to Maine's famous Baxter State Park right in the middle of the state. It's huge—more than 200,000 acres to explore! You'll find plenty more to do if you're not up for climbing the mountain—hiking, canoeing, camping (there are 10 campgrounds in the park to choose from), plus white-water rafting.

If you hear about the Allagash Wilderness Waterway, that's more than 90 miles of lakes, ponds, rivers, and streams running northwest from the park. It's popular for canoeing.

The city of Bangor is in the middle of this region.

Check out the giant Paul Bunyan statue—it's 31 feet tall! This part of Maine was once famous for logging—the trees would be cut down in the North Woods and milled and shipped from here—and Paul Bunyan was said to be a super logger from here.

Younger kids like the Maine Discovery Museum (74 Main St., Bangor; 207-262-7200; mainediscovery museum.org).

A MAINE KID SAYS

"We go camping at state parks and other places all over the state. I like it best if there is a pool or especially a lake, like Sebago Lake State Park and Lily Bay on Moosehead Lake, so we can go swimming and fishing and kayaking."
—Mike, 14, Freeport

All kids like the Cole Land Transportation Museum (405 Perry Rd., Bangor; 207-990-3600; colemuseum .org), which displays more than 200 old-fashioned vehicles from Maine—cars, fire engines, tractors, snow plows, even baby carriages.

You also aren't far from the University of Maine in Orono. Maine is famous for its night sky and the University's Maynard F. Jordan Planetarium invites you to take a look through a telescope on many Friday and Saturday nights (167 Rangeley Rd., Orono; 207-581-1341; astro.umaine.edu).

Moosehead Lake, deep in the Maine woods, is 40 miles long and is headquarters for water fun, whether you want to fish or boat. There's also mountain biking and rock climbing in this area. Maybe your family would want to go on a multi-day canoe trip? Local outfitters can take you!

A MAINE KID SAYS

"For a souvenir, I'd get something like a necklace with something I'd seen on it, like a moose, or something that reminds me of my trip. And if you are brave, try steamed clams or raw oysters while you are in Maine."
—Judy, 13, Portland

Visit the Moosehead Marine Museum (12 Lily Bay Rd., Greenville; 207-695-2716; katahdincruises.com) or take a cruise on the lake aboard a historic steamboat and learn what life was like here more than 100 years ago.

Of course, you have lots of rivers and lakes to choose from, including Sebago and Long Lakes, and the Rangeley Lakes Region. There are 10 lakes just within the town of Bridgton; climb to the summit of Pleasant Mountain and you can see 50! The trick is to just pick one area and stay awhile.

But the fun doesn't stop when it gets cold. Families come here for winter sports too. Have you ever been ice fishing?

A Super Trail

Could you hike 2,180 miles?

Every year, some 2,000 people try to hike the **Appalachian Trail** (AppalachianTrail.org) that passes through 14 states and is a National Scenic Trail. Millions from around the world visit the A.T. as it is known someplace between where it starts in Georgia and ends in the Maine Highlands, maybe hiking a mile or 2. You could hike 281 miles of it in Maine. Hikers stay in rustic, three-sided shelters along the trail, carrying their food. Their packs are heavy! Every year, many volunteers work to keep the trail maintained.

It takes about six months to hike the entire trail, starting in Georgia in the spring and ending in Maine in the fall, but only one in four who start make it to the end. Along the way, the hikers adopt nicknames like "Crumb-snatcher" or "Thunder Chicken." What's your trail nickname going to be?

{ **WHAT'S COOL?** Seeing moose, black bears, foxes, eagles, and more at the **Maine Wildlife Park** (56 Game Farm Rd., Route 26, Gray; 207-657-4977; maine.gov/ifw/education/wildlifepark)—a haven for animals who can no longer live in the wild.

Brake for Moose!

Watch out for moose!

They don't obey traffic signals. Early and late in the day, they wander roadsides, especially on logging roads in the Maine Highlands.

There are an estimated 75,000 moose in Maine—more than any other state except Alaska—which is why you see them on everything from sweatshirts to socks to water bottles and key chains.

The most moose are in the Western Lakes and Mountains, the Kennebec Valley, Maine Highlands, and Aroostook County.

In fall, you can see their antlers when they're most impressive; they'll shed them in November or December and grow new ones in the spring.

They like high grass and shrubs because they are so tall that lowering their head to the ground can be difficult.

Learn more about them on a Moose Safari with a company such as Maine Quest Adventures (2062 Medway Rd., Medway; 207-447-5011; mainequestadventures.com) or New England Outdoor Center (30 Twin Pines Rd., Millinocket, ME 04462; 800-766-7238; neoc.com).

If you see a moose, don't get too close! Though calves only weigh 30 pounds at birth, they can outrun people by the time they are five days old!

TELL THE ADULTS

Maine is about enjoying the outdoors, but there is plenty to learn in Augusta, the state capitol. Check out:

- The **Maine State Museum** (230 State St., Augusta; 207-287-2301; mainestatemuseum .org), which offers interactive exhibits showcasing Maine's history. It is part of a state government complex that includes the State House (check out the replica of the Liberty Bell!) and the Maine State Library.

- **Old Fort Western** (16 Cony St., Augusta; 207-626-2385; oldfortwestern.org) is the country's oldest remaining stockade fort. Costumed interpreters will help kids time travel back to the eighteenth century with hands-on demonstrations from musket drills to vinegar making.

DID YOU KNOW?

The pouch of skin that hangs from a moose's neck is called a bell.

A bull moose weighs over 1,000 pounds and his antlers span 6 feet!

WHAT'S COOL? Apple and pumpkin picking in Maine in the fall. Try **Douglas Mountain Orchard** (42 Orchard Rd.; 207-787-2745; douglashillorchard.wixsite.com) in Sebago or **Five Fields Farm** (720 S Bridgton Rd.; 207- 647-2425; fivefieldsski.com) in Bridgton.

- The **Samantha Smith Memorial**. Ten-year-old Samantha wrote to Uri Andropov, the Premier of the Soviet Union, in 1982, confiding her fears of nuclear war. He invited her and her family to visit Russia and the event was considered a step toward peace efforts. Sadly, she died in a plane crash in 1985.

- **The Theater at Monmouth** (796 Main St., Monmouth; 207-933-9999; theateratmonmouth .org) not only is home to The Shakespearean Theater of Maine but also showcases children's theater in a restored 100-year-old building.

- The **Children's Discovery Museum** (171 Capitol St. #2, Augusta; 207-622-2209; childrensdiscovery museum.org) is designed for kids through age five complete with a Kennebec River room (the museum overlooks the river), multi-cultural music center, and tree house/nature center.

Go Fishing

It's about the fishing, not the catching!

But hopefully, you'll catch something, especially since Maine is famous for its fishing. The Kennebec River is best known for striped bass and bluefish; Moosehead Lake for trout. There's also salmon fishing. If your family loves to fish, you might want to stay at a traditional fishing camp. The **Maine Sporting Camps Association** (mainesporting camps.com) can help you find one. Remind your parents to get a fishing license. Here are a few fishing tips:

- Fish early in the morning or late in the evening.

- Don't wear bright colors—you don't want the fish to see you!

- Don't let your shadow fall on the water.

- Don't stay in one place too long. Fish a spot for a little while and move on.

A MAINE KID SAYS

"My family has a camp on Rangely Lake (in the western mountains of Maine), so we go there a lot in the summer. We've got kayaks and spend most of our time out fishing and exploring, but there are lots of mountains to hike in the area if you like hiking. Rangely has some good restaurants and shops. We usually go out in the early evening looking for moose along the logging roads. They are pretty common up there."
—Ashley, 11, Portland

{ WHAT'S COOL? **The Maine Whoopie Pie Festival** (mainewhoopiepiefestival.com) held in June in Dover-Foxcroft. Bakers from around the country compete for the best whoopie pie, a very popular Maine snack.

MAINE MANIA CROSSWORD PUZZLE

The answers to this crossword puzzle are all mentioned in this chapter.

Across

3. The first town in Maine over the bridge from New Hampshire
8. The capital of Maine
9. Tall towers with lights that helped ships to shore
11. The name of Maine's largest lake
12. Native Americans who lived in Maine for thousands of years

Down

1. Maine town famous for its outlets and L.L. Bean
2. The giant store in Freeport with indoor trout pond that never closes
4. Portland's minor league baseball team
5. You may need Binoculars to see them in the sky
6. A giant famous lumberjack character said to have been born in Maine
7. Yummy snack famous in Maine with two pieces of chocolate cake with frosting in between
10. What is the easternmost state in the continental USA

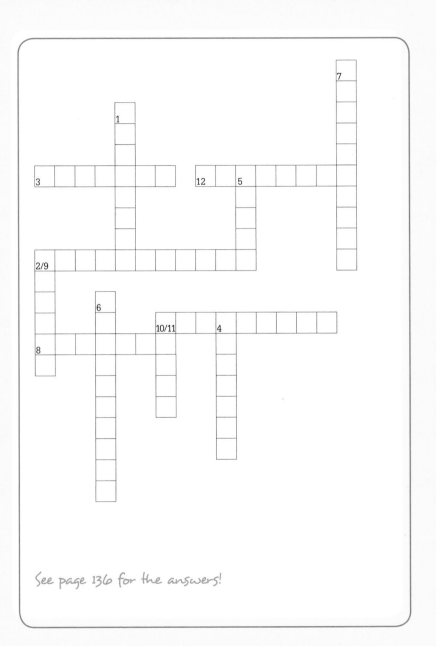

See page 136 for the answers!

10

Winter in Maine—
The Fun Continues

There's no feeling like it!

Picture this: You're flying down a snow-covered mountain on skis or a snowboard, zooming past trees and grownups—and probably your mom and dad!

That's after you've had a few lessons, of course! Some kids start skiing before they've even gone to kindergarten. They make it seem really easy, but skiing and riding is a lot harder than it looks. That's why you shouldn't try to head off on some expert slope before you have the technique down.

A MAINE KID SAYS
"I love ice skating at the outdoor rink in Yarmouth when the Christmas lights are everywhere."
—Missy, 10, Yarmouth

Ski schools shouldn't really be called "school" because they're so much fun and give you the chance to meet kids from all over the world. Together, you'll learn the skills to conquer snow-covered peaks safely.

These days, snow resorts have special just-for-kids areas on the mountains, complete with mascots as well as activities when the lifts have closed—tubing, ice skating, broomball games, bonfires, snow cat tours, ziplines, big hot tubs, and festivals all winter. You can try something you've never done—take a snowshoe walk on top of the mountain or soak in the hot mineral springs at some resorts.

DID YOU KNOW?

There are more than 575 downhill skiing and snowboarding trails in Maine.

WHAT'S COOL? Being one of the first ones down a ski slope after a fresh snowfall—called "first tracks."

There are plenty of places to have fun in the snow in Maine. Sunday River (15 S. Ridge Rd., Newry; 207-824-3000; sundayriver.com) has eight interconnected mountain peaks with 135 trails and five terrain parks, including the longest half-pipe in the east and "Who-Ville" for beginners. You won't get bored! Sugarloaf (5092 Access Rd., Carrabassett Valley, 800-THE LOAF; sugarloaf.com) promises the only above-tree-line skiing in the East with views of Vermont, New Hampshire, and Canada. Welcome to the biggest ski area east of the Rockies with plenty of terrain to suit everyone, including a beginner terrain park

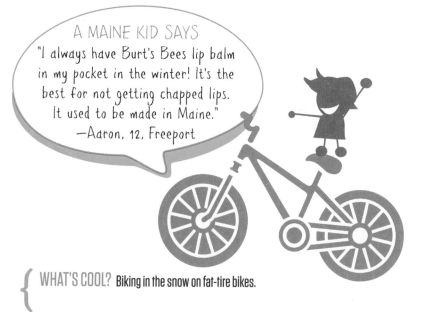

A MAINE KID SAYS
"I always have Burt's Bees lip balm in my pocket in the winter! It's the best for not getting chapped lips. It used to be made in Maine."
—Aaron, 12, Freeport

{ WHAT'S COOL? Biking in the snow on fat-tire bikes.

on the popular Whiffletree area of the mountain. Camden Snow Bowl (20 Barnestown Rd., Camden; 207-236-3438; camdensnowbowl.com) may be small, but it's famous for its 400-foot toboggan run. Have you ever been on a toboggan? Get ready to go fast!

How about dog sledding? There are places in Maine to give that a try too—like Maine Dog Sledding Adventures (207-731-8888; mainedogsledding.com).

Many kids learn winter sports at places such as Mt. Abram Ski Area (308 Howe Hill Rd., Greenwood; 207-875-5000; mtabram.com), just outside of Bethel in Greenwood with its three terrain

A MAINE KID SAYS

"I like walking downtown during snowstorms. There's hardly any cars around or people out. It's like having the whole city to yourself. Sometimes I meet the news crews out getting film."
—Natika, 14, Portland

parks where you can practice tricks; Black Mountain Ski Resort (39 Glover Rd., Rumford; 207-364-8977; skiblack mountain.org) in Rumford, especially known for its cross-country skiing; and Bigrock Mountain (37 Graves Rd., Mars Hill; 207-425-6711; bigrockmaine.com) in Mars Hill.

Have you ever been skiing after dark when the ski hill is all lit up? It's really fun!

Kids in Maine love all winter sports—ice hockey and skating, tubing and sledding, cross-country skiing and snowshoeing—sometimes right out their back doors, a

DID YOU KNOW?

Skiing has been around a lot longer than snowboarding. It wasn't until 1984 that a US ski resort—Stratton in Vermont—agreed to allow snowboarders access to its slopes, thanks to Jake Burton Carpenter's efforts. He is the founder of Burton and first made snowboards in his garage and sold them out of his car in Vermont. Today there are only three resorts in the country that don't allow snowboarders—Alta and Deer Valley in Utah and Mad River Glen in Vermont.

local park or a place such as Baxter State Park or Acadia National Park. The park will be an entirely different place without the summer crowds and covered in snow!

Lots of Maine families go snowmobiling—there are thousands of trails that wind through forests and towns.

Get outside in the winter and enjoy!

A MAINE KID SAYS

"My whole family goes snowmobiling. There are lots of trails that clubs take care of, and some that people just make themselves. We take tons of food and water with us because you get really hungry and usually you're a long way from a store."

—Dez, 14, Freeport

TELL THE ADULTS

Snow sports are expensive, but lessons are a good value for the money. Let the pros teach the kids! They've had special training and know the most fun spots on the mountain. Here are some ways to keep costs down:

- Early season and late season often offer the best lodging deals with discounted lift tickets. You can also find discounted tickets on sites such as Lifetopia.com (liftopia.com).

- Kids who are in fifth, sixth, or seventh grade and live in Maine are eligible for a **WinterKids** passport (winterkids.org). But you must apply in advance. There are free and discounted lift tickets, opportunities for cross-country skiing, ice skating, and snow tubing, as well as lessons and rentals at 50 areas all over Maine. There are also special WinterKids Family Days.

- WinterKids.org offers a FunPass for Maine Kids from preschool through fourth grade to try cross-country skiing and snowshoeing on groomed trails free.

- There are many opportunities for discounted and free lessons and lifts in January during **Learn a Snow Sport Month** (skiandsnowboard month.org).

- You can save money if you book lodging and lifts together.

- You might try a different kind of adventure—snowshoeing or cross-country skiing and staying in eco lodges on 80 miles of trails (mainehuts.org); The Appalachian Mountain Club (outdoors.org) also offers back-country, kid-friendly experiences in the heart of the AMC's 100-Mile Wilderness Conservation Lands. And someone cooks for you!

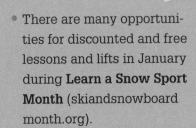

Snow Carving 101

Got a big plastic garbage can? A big cardboard box will also do.

   Fill either with snow and stomp it down really hard. Turn the container upside down or cut off the cardboard and you've got a block of snow. Let it freeze overnight and you're ready to become a snow carver.

   Get out cheese graters, putty knives, spoons, and paint scrapers—whatever you have will work. Pick an animal shape, a flower, or something else you'd like to build. Use a small toy or a picture to guide you.

   What is your masterpiece going to look like?

DID YOU KNOW?

Before modern refrigerators, huge blocks of ice were sawed from Maine's frozen lakes and rivers and carried to distant ports to keep food cold. That was called ice harvesting.

Lids on Kids

Got your helmet?

A lot of snow resorts insist you wear one when you take lessons to learn to ski or ride because you are safer. You'll stay warmer and drier, too, with a helmet on your head. Once you slap stickers on it, people will know all the mountains you've seen! Wear your helmet whenever you head out to the slopes. Your parents should wear them too. Check out Lids on Kids (lidsonkids.org) for fun games.

Gear Up

The wrong clothes can ruin a fun day on the slopes. To be comfortable and safe, you will need:

- to dress in layers, starting with a base layer that will wick moisture away;

- socks made to wear under ski boats or snowboard boots;

- waterproof pants, jacket, and mittens;

- a helmet;

- goggles or good sunglasses with UV protection (definitely goggles if it's snowing!);

- sunscreen in the mountains (you're closer to the sun, which is especially strong when it reflects off the snow);

- a healthy snack in your pocket.

Know the Code

- Always ski in control.

- The people ahead of you have the right of way. Whenever starting downhill or merging, look uphill and yield.

- Stop in a safe place for you and others, not in the middle of a slope.

- Observe signs and warnings and keep off closed trails.

- Look for the colors on the trail signs: Green trails are easiest, blue is more difficult, and black is for experts. Ski on the trails where you feel the most comfortable. It's more fun.

- Stop when you're tired or cold. That's when people tend to get hurt.

{ WHAT'S COOL? A young instructor who can show you his or her favorite places on the mountain to do tricks on skis and snowboards.

Ski Patrol

The **National Ski Patrol** makes skiing safer. You can pick ski patrollers out on the mountain by the white cross on their parkas and the first-aid belts around their waists. You'll see them helping skiers who have been hurt or have gotten lost. If you get lost, look for them or an instructor with a class. They'll help you. Ski patrollers range in age from teenagers to grandfathers. Many are volunteers. The National Ski Patrol was founded in the 1930s by New York businessman Charles Minot Dole after he broke his ankle skiing—and had to get down the mountain himself. The National Ski Patrol has become the largest winter rescue organization in the world, saving many lives. Say thanks next time you see a ski patrol member.

DID YOU KNOW?

A storm called a "Nor'easter" can drop 10 or more inches of snow in one day. The northern interior of Maine gets 90 to 110 inches of snow a year, but you'll find much less along the coast.

FILL IN THE BLANKS

Can you fill in the missing spots to spell out winter activities you might enjoy in Maine?

Do__nh__ll sk__i__g

S__ows__oei__g

Sn__w __ub__ng

D__g __led__ing

S__ow__oar__ing

I__e s__at__ng

S__ow__ob__ling

C__o__s co__ntry s__ii__g

S__o__ car__ing

See page 137 for the answers!

{ **WHAT'S COOL?** Trying a new kind of fun in the snow—snowshoeing under the moon, snow biking, taking a ride on a dog sled, or tubing down a giant track.

Answer Keys

Maine Word Scramble (p. 11)

Lobster

Paddleboarding

Moose

Beaches

LL Bean

Blueberries

Mountains

Augusta

Skiing

Ocean

Maine Word Search! (p. 23)

N	U	B	B	L	E	L	I	G	H	T	F	B
S	U	N	S	C	R	E	E	N	A	O	N	L
C	F	K	I	T	T	E	R	Y	G	U	A	U
V	A	C	A	T	I	O	N	L	A	N	D	E
E	L	N	P	D	I	V	U	T	M	T	I	B
T	Y	O	R	K	B	F	M	L	E	C	A	E
M	U	M	B	R	E	L	L	A	N	R	O	R
O	A	T	Y	S	A	M	R	D	T	H	T	R
O	I	I	P	J	T	C	E	Y	I	R	D	I
S	D	R	M	T	Y	E	L	Z	C	X	T	E
E	F	E	T	I	L	A	R	S	U	N	V	S
B	I	N	O	C	U	L	A	R	S	Q	P	N

Connect the dots (p. 37)

Lobster

Matching Famous Mainers (p. 51)

C   Rachel Carson
D   Leon Leonwood Bean
A   Henry Wadsworth Longfellow
B   George H. W. Bush

Maine Decoder (p. 63)

Sno<u>w</u>

Mount Kata<u>h</u>din

Old <u>O</u>rchard Beach   Free<u>p</u>ort

L<u>o</u>bster   Stephen K<u>i</u>ng

National <u>P</u>ark   Blueb<u>e</u>rry

L<u>i</u>ghthouse

Moos<u>e</u>   <u>W</u> <u>h</u> <u>o</u> <u>o</u> <u>p</u> i e <u>P</u> i <u>e</u>

Whale Matching (p. 77)

Flukes   the horizontal lobes of a whale's tail

Breach   when a whale jumps out of the water and lands on its side or back

Spyhopping   when a whale pokes its nose out of the water to look around

Bow-riding   when a whale positions itself to be lifted and pushed by moving water

Tail slap   when a whale slaps its tail flukes on the water's surface

Maine Maze! (p. 89)

Connect the Dots (p. 103)
Moose

Maine Mania Crossword Puzzle (p. 116)

Across

3 Kittery
8 Augusta
9 Lighthouses
11 Moosehead
12 Wabanaki

Down

1 Freeport
2 LL Bean
4 Sea Dogs
5 Birds
6 Paul Bunyan
7 Whoopie Pie
10 Maine

Fill in the Blanks (p. 133)

Downhill skiing

Snowshoeing

Snow tubing

Dog sledding

Snowboarding

Ice skating

Snowmobiling

Cross country skiing

Snow carving

Index